101 VIEWS
OF THE VICTORIA FALLS

BY ROBERT ZULU

Copyright © 2014 by Dr. Robert Zulu. 633798

ISBN: Softcover   978-1-4990-8772-7
        EBook   978-1-4990-8771-0

All rights reserved. No part of this book may be reproduced or transmitted in any form or by any means, electronic or mechanical, including photocopying, recording, or by any information storage and retrieval system, without permission in writing from the copyright owner.

Printed in the United States of America by BookMasters, Inc
Ashland OH
November 2014
50006754

Rev. date: 10/22/2014

To order additional copies of this book, contact:
Xlibris
0800-056-3182
www.xlibrispublishing.co.uk
Orders@Xlibrispublishing.co.uk

Dedication

To my mother Tomaida and late father Gilizani who moved on to Livingstone town in Zambia where I was introduce to this natural wonder; the Victoria Falls. Most of all, to the Almighty God who made it possible for me to have life in abundance through Jesus Christ.

Acknowledgement

I want to acknowledge the support I received from my family and friends without which this work was not going to be complete. My wife Prisca for her patience, Mayase and Tomaida for helping to proof read the manuscript and helping with taking images, Mumba, Mannaseh and Zewelanji for the encouragement.

To professor Kasonde Bowa for giving me the inspiration to put my ideas on paper and friends and colleagues. To all of you great and small, a big thank you!

Table of Contents

Introduction 1
Dr. David Livingstone 2
From a Distance 4
The Look out Tree ("Up-side down" Tree) 6
The Lookout Platform 7
The Photographic Trail 9
The Palm Groove Trail 13
The "Boiling Pot" 16
The Eastern Cataract 17
The Knife Edge Bridge 19
The Knife Edge Island Trail 20
The Geological Strata 22
The Picnic (Up Stream) Trail 23
The "Bird's Eye View" 24
The Victoria Falls Bridge 25
Viewing the Falls in the "Bat's Position" 27
The Western Cataracts 28
Viewing at Position-2 29
The Devil's Cataract 30
Livingstone Island View 32
The Danger point 33
End of the Western Cataracts 34
Lunar Night View of the Falls 34
The Sunset View of the Falls 34
The Flora of the Victoria Falls 35
Animals of the Victoria Falls 36
Other Points of Interest 38
Finale 39
Glossary 40

Introduction

The Victoria Falls also called 'The Smoke that Thunders!' is about the largest curtain of water dropping 9 600 cubic meters of water per second down a series of basalt of gorges at the highest peak of the year. It is about 1708meters (5603 ft) wide and 100 meters (328ft) deep down the canyon.

Rising up is an iridescent spray that can be viewed about 30 km away along the road from Lusaka to Livingstone, in Zambia and 50km from Bulawayo road to Victoria Falls down in Zimbabwe. The water volume varies between the wet rainy season when it is very high and the hot dry season when it is low. It is one of the world's seven wonders which should be on your 'bucket list'.

The falls is located in the Mosi-oa-Tunya national park (Zambia) and Victoria national park (Zimbabwe) along the Zambezi river. It stands at an altitude of 915m above sea level and the gorges are a breeding site for some endangered bird and wild animal species. It is also residence for a lot of wild animals enjoying the rich green vegetation of the "Rain forest".

Forming the political border between Zambia to the north and Zimbabwe to the south, hosted by Livingstone city in Zambia and Victoria falls town in Zimbabwe. The site is a hive of tourist activities with several hotels, lodges and guest houses on both sides of the border. The common language for communication on both side of the border is English. The currency of trade in Zambia is Kwacha and the United States dollars in Zimbabwe.

Getting around can be by taxi or mini bus from your lodge/hotel to the falls and is safe to walk around. Some lodges are a walking distance to the falls. If you desire to hire a car, there are several companies that offer the service. Feel free to move around and visit as many places as you want by whatever means of transport you prefer. Enjoy the Falls and refresh your mind and body.

Hope this book will be helpful to making the most out of your visit to the Victoria Falls whether you are a returning guest or a first time visitor. Plan your visit and use your time wisely.

Dr. David Livingstone

It is only appropriate to start with the man associated with the falls, whose statue is erected on the Zambian and Zimbabwean sides of the falls. **The man Livingstone; cities, colleges, schools and roads where named after. The man who explored terrain, rivers of central, southern and east Africa.**

That man was no other than Dr David Livingstone: missionary, explorer, and anti-slavery advocate born on 19th March 1813 in Scotland and died on 1st May1873 at Chitambo mission in Zambia. He was the first white man to view the Mosi-oa-Tunya falls and named it after the Queen of United Kingdom Queen Victoria. The local people used and still call it Mosi-oa-Tunya falls meaning 'The smoke that thunders'.

As an explorer, one of his missions was to discover the source of the Nile river and whether he succeeded or not is debatable. The least we can do is applaud him for efforts. He succeeded in opening up central Africa to other explorers who came after him And used his maps and knowledge to further his works which he pioneered to further his works which he pioneered. Amongst other things, he was also the first white man to visit lake Malawi and explore the Zambezi river.

Dr Livingstone is also remembered for his missionary work, introducing Christianity to tribes in Central and southern Africa. He treated natives with respect and fought a crusade against slavery as a result, Arabs did not like him. He did his best to convert the local native population to Christianity but this was not easy for him.

In spite of these and many other challenges, he opened up opportunities for other missionaries to bring in Christianity and western education. He himself considered his missionary work to be far of greater value than his exploratory work of looking for the source of the Nile river.

His wife unfortunately died of malaria in Malawi and her body was buried there. His personal assistants Chuma and Sushi are remembered for their dedication to Livingstone staying with him when many had deserted him, even after he died, they transported his remains to the shore in Tanzania for onward transportation to the United Kingdom where they were put to rest.

The detailed works and life of David Livingstone can be found in the Livingstone Museum.

From a Distance

An appetizing sight of the Victoria falls along the road to Livingstone from the northern side can be seen as a plum of clouds rising from the ground. The view is much exciting when the sky is clear. This can be sighted as far as 30 km from Livingstone town. A similar plum of clouds rising from the ground can be sighted along the Bulawayo road to Victoria Falls town as far as 50km away.

From this distance, there is no thunderous sound of water pounding the ground as it hits the gorge down the falls because the falls is too far for the sound. You may want to take pictures but no one stops as the sighting of the falls acts as a spur to drive on and arrive. Stopping and taking pictures at this point is more like time wasting and everyone has the itch to move on and see the source of this plum of smoke. Whatever you decide, the sight of the falls at this point is the "starter" before the main meal.

Very few people have the patience to stop at the Lay-bye either in Zimbabwe or Zambia to start taking pictures at this distance. It is like a dream to come true and no one wants to wait just incase this is just smoke from a burning bush. This is the "Smoke that Thunders"(Mosi-oa- Tunya) appropriately named by the Toka leyas. So momentum is gathered and the journey goes on at full throttle.

It's a sight that may also be mistaken for "smoke" from a burning bush except that this smoke seems to be producing a thunderous sound as you draw near the sight.

As you approach the Livingstone town on the Zambian side, the cloud gathers size and so the sound also increases in loudness. When you reach Livingstone town, you still have 10km to the falls. On the Zimbabwean side, you also have to pass through the town and the distance is much less to the falls on this side. Drive with care as you pass through the game parks on both sides. Look out for animals particularly elephants crossing the road.

The Look out Tree ("Up-side down" Tree)

This view from the Baobab tree locally named the upside down tree because of the leafless twigs which look like roots. It is as if the tree is set upside down. This road is the Mukuni Village road leading to the official residence of Chief Mukuni who presides over the Toka Leya tribe. The village has its own attractions and is about 20 minutes drive from this point.

The view of the falls at this point is excellent and can be sighted from the northeast side of the falls. The falls will be seen at 09:00clock position. To get to this point, drive towards the falls from Livingstone town, take a left turn opposite the Royal Sun hotel, cross the rail line and drive for about 200metres towards Mukuni village and you will see a large Baobab tree with a stair case leading to the viewing point.

The space between twigs from the tree forms the window through which a magnificent view of the curtain of spray of the falls at an oblique position. At this point the Zambezi can be seen as a river basin flowing from the northwest while Livingstone town is at 12:00clock position. West of the falls is the Victoria falls town in Zimbabwe.

The Lookout Platform

To get to the **Lookout** tree from the **Viewing platform,** take the unpaved road south and drive for 4.2km following the directions. Passing through a rich savannah bush with a lot of Acacia trees and plenty of birds' nests hanging on branches on the trees along the roadside, you will enjoy the beautiful flora on the land.

Use the side steel support as you climb the 2.5 metres staircase to the platform specially built for viewing. From this viewing point, you will be viewing the Falls from the southern side and the falls is seen as a wide curtain of mist rising to form clouds. The falls is at 11:00clock position. It is a magnificent sight to behold regardless of the cloud cover. The view from this sight is all year round but best between March and November when the water level is at the highest peak.

Farther on, directly north, the city of Livingstone is visible as a cluster of silver reflection of light from the iron roofs. At night dotted lights from street lights are seen in straight line beautifully lined up. Directly to the west, is the Victoria Falls town in Zimbabwe seen as scattered buildings popping up in a thick beautiful vegetation of natural trees.

Immediately between the curtain of rising spray and the viewing platform, you will see the electric high voltage transmission power lines coming up from the generator producing electricity supplying power to Livingstone city , Victoria falls town and beyond.

The gorge continues from the north curving to the west and then south. This is a site for a gorge swing for the strong hearted to stimulate the adrenaline. The gorge swing can be accessed by turning immediately right after crossing the rail line on the road to the Lookout Tree. This will be discussed under **Other Points of Interest** further on in this book.

The Photographic Trail

The title of the trail says it all!. Bring out all your cameras, from mobile phone cameras to the high resolution professional cameras. There is less water spray with wide paths for safety and clear barriers. There is enough light most of the year and your flash on your camera can be turned off, depending on the weather.

To get on to the trail, pass through the entry point just opposite the curio shops and then, turn left following the trail next to the fence. Follow this path and it will lead you to the photographic trail.

You will be seeing the view from the southern side and it will be on your right. On your left is the road to the Victoria falls bridge and the Victoria falls town in Zimbabwe. Keep on the path and several viewing stations are provided and secured with barriers for your safety to allow you take your pictures without danger.

An ordinary camera can do as sated but for distant objects, a camera with zoom lens will help you capture objects with good clarity without you moving to the edge. Most of the trail is dry, with no slippery rocks making it easy to walk and take pictures safely.

The following are some of the things you will be able to do or see;

1. Bungee jumpers at a closer view and even take videos as they jump.
2. Train, cars and people crossing the Livingstone bridge
3. In a distance with a good pair of binoculars, you can see tourists on the Zimbabwe side walking towards the Danger point.
4. The Boiling Pot can be seen if you look down the gorge on your right. Again a pair of binoculars or powerful lens will capture excited people who have made it down the gorge to the falls.
5. Beautiful carpet of green flora covering the rocks and sides of the chasm with the falls constantly spraying it.
6. Different species of trees and creepers
7. People crossing the knife edge bridge soaked to the skin or in rain coats.

Botanists and alike will have an opportunity to study this 'rainy forest' with the uncut trees and creepers. One of the reasons the area was fenced was to keep elephants away from destroying the vegetation.

The Palm Groove Trail

As you come out of the Photographic trail, the Palm groove trail is immediately to your left down the gorge and clearly labeled with an arrow written Boiling Pot. A gentle walk will take 15minutes to the boiling pot from this point and twice as long coming up for a distance of about 120meters. Rest benches are provided along the trail.

Make use of the camera; both short and long lens to take shots of birds, monkeys, the Livingstone bridge and of course the Boiling pot. Along the way, ¾ down the trail is a head pond siphon scour dissipater.

Carrying one or two bottles of water is advised but not essential. The slope is steep and rocks have sharp edges, hence take care as you climb up and descend down the slope. The trail is clear and has a staircase in some portions done to ease the walk. Side supports are provided where the slope is very steep.

The vegetation is made up of tall, short palm trees and interlacing indigenous creepers. The air is cool, refreshing and re-energizing. The noise above is that of indigenous birds and the thundering sound of the pounding water as it hits the bottom of the falls. It is an experience that words cannot describe. Excellent place to study the natural vegetation of the falls.

Birds though high up on trees can be seen using a pair of binoculars. Species of different birds like the common sparrow and the sun birds are worth watching. Crow are not uncommon in this habitat.

Large reptiles are absent may be because of the large volume of visitors. Snakes are very rarely seen but small lizards and Geckos are common, usually seen on the rock surfaces or hiding in the cracks.

Obvious in the Palm groove trail are primates. Sometimes snatching food from your hands. It is not uncommon to finds food bins turned over by these mammals are they look for left over foods to eat.

Take time climbing up to view the rich thick green vegetation forming a carpet covering the sides of the gorge. This view forms a complimentary sight to the falls. Most of the trail as stated earlier is dry except at its end as you approach the boiling pot. Mind your step, the trail is covered by natural rocks some of which may be sharp. Use support rails when the trail is sloppy or slippery. These have been provided to make your walk safe and comfortable.

Rest on the benches provided. This is an opportunity to meditate and reflect on the natural wonder. There is no need to race up the trail unless you are a professional athlete. You will have unnecessary aches of muscles for days making your holidays unpleasant.

The "Boiling Pot"

Passing through the Palm Groove trail, at the end, you will see right in front of you a body of water going round and round with 'steam' rising up, hence the name 'Boiling Pot'.

The swirl of water (Boiling pot) is due to a backflow of water coming from the falls as it reaches resistance from the rock beneath. The water is cool, clear and refreshing. The scenery is splendid and gives you that feeling of winning after passing through the steep Palm groove trail. The green vegetation around, a breeze of cool mist, a sight of water spinning around and a thunderous deafening sound in the background, is difficult to describe in words.

It is a splendid view in and of its self, with Bungee jumpers 'flying' down from up the bridge as if they were small birds falling into the river but spring back up the bridge. One jumper narrating her Story, stated that it was one of her 'bucket list' to come from London and do a bungee jump from the Victoria falls bridge. "Now that I have done it, I feel complete".

White water rafting sport starts from here and can be watched from the knife edge bridge, the photographic trail and the Victoria falls bridge. This is another adrenaline raising sport not for the simple hearted. Teams congregate and paddle the rafts down the stream. Each member of the team can testify of the adrenaline rush that makes the game exciting.

The Eastern Cataract

As you can tell from the name, this is the most eastern part of the falls and is the deepest side of the gorge. It can be viewed from three main points. The east most, which is usually dry, offers an awesome sight. The second view of the eastern cataract is directly in front of the rain coat hire stand. It is dry and can easily be accessed up to this point wheelchair friendly.

This is one of the most photographed spots of the falls because of its location and the beautiful view it offers. To view the eastern cataract from the western side proceed down the trail with appropriate rubber shoes and rain coat. Remember from this, protect electronic gadgets from water, you will be sprayed with water from this point onwards.

Enjoy the serene walk in the green rain forest with a ground shacking thunderous sound of water pounding the gorge. What a contrast! You will experience an unmatched tranquility that will harmonize your soul and body. If you have problems in finding a perfect natural wonder that affects your body, heart and soul, this one will definitely this one has the perfect facets.

The Knife Edge Bridge

To cross or not to cross the knife edge bridge, that's the question! "If I do not cross the bridge, I will miss out on the beautiful view from the head land…" That's what everyone who comes to this point seems to be contemplating. This is seen from the way they hesitate as they stand looking at the bridge. The fear does not come from the structure of the bridge, but rather from the position of the bridge passing through a chasm too deep to see its bottom. It gives you the feeling of being at 'The edge of a knife'.

The bridge was built in 1968 by the Ministry of Works and Supply of the Zambian government. It is 40metres long and 130cm wide. It has secure steel supports, the floor is completely sealed steel sheet. It rains incessantly making the floor slippery but with rubber shoes you will have a secure grip. Again, take care of your electronic equipment, especially cameras and watches, unless they are waterproof, they will get soaked and malfunction. Take extra care of toddlers, these are dangerous areas.

A beautiful rainbow can be seen on the southern side of the bridge like an arch in full seven colours. The northern side of the bridge is covered by a crowd of mist spraying from the gorge to the sky making photography difficult unless with special cameras and electronic gadgets that are waterproof.

Immediately after crossing the bridge, remove your camera from the safety of the plastic/waterproof bag and enjoy the view as you look backward towards the bridge. At this point you are now entering the Head land.

The Knife Edge Island Trail

After crossing the bridge, experience the feeling of freedom. Look back at the bridge think again why you hesitated crossing. The experience of crossing the bridge is like walking on a knife edge. This experience may be helpful in character building for those that need help to build their character.

Take the trail on your right and you will be walking along the Knife edge Island trail. You should be able to see the Rainbow falls, the Danger point, the Horse shoe falls, and the Livingstone island in a distance if the spray does not form a thick cloud. On the southern side of the island, the Victoria falls bridge and the Geological strata is clearly visible all year round.

The **Rainbow Falls** is one of the spectacular views to look out for. The Spray of water rising from the gorge as a curtain breaks into small droplets and the sun rays passing through the droplets splits light into the seven colours of the rainbow; Red, Orange, Yellow, Green, Blue, Indigo and Violet. You should be able to see all these beautiful colours of the rainbow on a good sunny day.

The **Danger point** on the Zambian side and the Zimbabwean side is actually the same area separated by a deep chasm. It appears that this area was connected to the Zimbabwean side. Looking down from the sky, you can see a strip of land remaining which was an Isthmus connecting both lands.

The **Horse shoe falls** is seen further on just before the Livingstone island sometimes blurred due to the spray of water. Its characteristic shape is that of a shoe of a horse. I am sure this feature will be eroded as time passes. Make haste to view this feature whilst it is in view.

The **Livingstone Island** is not very clear from this point. You need a good pair of binoculars. It will be discussed when looking at the western cataracts.

The **flora** on the island is green with broad leafy trees interlaced with long creepers hanging from slender but strong trees. From lofty high on trees, occasionally you will hear the sweet songs of birds drowned in contrast by the thunderous sounds of the falls. The birds on this habitat must have developed extraordinary hearing sense to be able to communicate with each other in the midst of the drowning sound of the falls.

The Geological Strata

The southern side of the headland offers magnificent view of the geological strata. Lack of the water spray has left the rock dry, without vegetation showing the layers of soil with different colours signifying different layers of rock formation with its own message. Details of the rock formation are outside the scope of this book but suffice to say that it casts its own beauty worth admiring.

If you are a geologist, or an archaeologist, you will find this view purely academic and professional. For the rest of us this is a wondrous God's creation worth appreciating. This rock appearance has attempted to explain the falls formation and likewise predict the movement and future position of the water falls.

The Picnic (Up Stream) Trail

To go to upstream, turn right when you are facing the Eastern Cataract and follow the trail. This is in fact a short walk up stream along the river bank. It is advisable to take this trail after you have been soaked so that the dry heat along the trail will in no time dry your clothes up.

The trail helps you to reflect on the beauty and wonder that you been exposed to or simply, unwind. From the trail, you will be able to see the Livingstone island. Though the water is attractive for swimming, do not swim at this point or any other point as the current may be very strong and carry you down to the falls.

From October to December, the water level is low and you can walk up-to the Livingstone Island jumping over on rocks. Take care as you step on rocks. Some rocks have sharp edges and may be slippery.

Although the area is called picnic area, eating is not allowed because of monkeys and baboons. The animals are known to snatch food and would be difficult to control if one held a picnic. These animals are very curious but do not harm people in normal circumstances.

The "Bird's Eye View"

I wonder what birds think of this wonder as they fly over the falls from the sky. Try this by using either a micro aircraft or a helicopter flight or even the big plane. During descent at the Livingstone international airport, sometimes the pilot lowers the plane tilting it enabling passengers to get a 'bird's eye view of the falls'.

The whole falls can be seen starting with the Zambezi river, then the water as it falls into the series of cataract, the cloud of mist rising from the gorge, the knife edge bridge, the Livingstone bridge and then a series of gorges meandering round like a snake carrying with it a large column of water.

This is a view "without borders"! No passport or visa requirements but full, complete and perfect.

The Victoria Falls Bridge

An Engineering masterpiece of the time built by Cleveland Bridge and Engineering company of the United Kingdom. The bridge is 198metres long with an arch of 156 metres and is 128 metres above the water level. This master piece was part of Sir Cecil Rhodes plan of connecting Cape town to Cairo up north in Egypt.

Officially opened on 5th September 1905 by Professor George Darwin (Astronomer), grandson of Charles Darwin. At the time it was the highest in the world. Pedestrians, trains and cars all pass through the bridge and is an important, political, and geographical structure between the two countries.

Deliberately positioned to allow tourists to experience the spray. As such provides a beautiful and spectacular view of the falls. From here, with a pair of binoculars, down to the right facing north, you will see the water swirling round the boiling pot. Tourists can occasionally be seen sitting on the rocks relaxing in the cool spray from the falls contemplating on the astounding sight of the boiling pot.

Straight north, the water can be seen coming down from the Zimbabwean side and Zambian side proceeding to the boiling pot where they spin. On the right and left of the cliff, is a thick green vegetation green the whole round. Right on the bridge, mid point is the Bungee jumping site providing one of the highest points in the world for this sport.

Viewing the Falls in the "Bat's Position"

Imagine looking at the water falls with head down and feet up! Flying down like a bird to the river below at pulling speed of gravity and end up with your feet up like a Bat. In this position, looking at the falls and admiring the beauty and splendor in the 'Bats position' is beyond what words can describe. Take pictures if you can but most of all, experience the adventure.

Hang on the ropes swinging from side to side and let the spray soak you to the skin. At this moment your heart will be racing like a horse but yet enjoying every second of the dive and view. You may be able to see the rainbow depending on the position of the sun rays. Look at the vegetation on sides of the cliff, look at the water below, look at the spray rising up. The flora looks like a thick carpet of green leaves and fungi. The air you will be breathing is cool and will calm all your nerves down.

There are no better words to explain this experience than to get onto the ropes and take the jump yourself, of course under supervision. No wonder people travel thousands of kilometres crossing land and sea to just have this bungee jump experience.

The Western Cataracts

The western cataracts are those that can be better viewed from the Zimbabwean side. You need to do cross border formalities and enter the Zimbabwean side of the falls.

When you enter the gate, take the left trail passing through viewing point number-2 clearly labelled. Walk for about 100metres up stream. What you will be seeing are the western cataracts. You will clearly see a large volume of water forcefully undermining the edge of the earth underneath. Geologists tell us that the falls is gradually moving westward.

There is no spray at this point and the vegetation is dry woodland with tall natural trees, like the Crocodile bark , Bird plum and Milk berry trees, which are scattered around. The grass is very short, green or brown depending on the season of the year.

There is a tall secure fence to keep away overzealous intruders and if you have toddlers around, remember to keep watch over them. Restrain them using specially made straps if you have to. Rescue missions in the deep gorges are not practical.

Viewing at Position-2

At this position, there is minimal or no mist at all. It is a good position for taking great pictures. The falls is seen sideways from the west. The bottom is not visible and is dangerous to try and visualise it.

Walk on east wards and you will see a staircase going down. Walk down the secure path down the staircase and you will see a marvelous large column of water fall down the gorge continuously. A beautiful rainbow is cast usually on your right depending on the position of the sun.

The Devil's Cataract

The Devil's cataract can be better viewed from position-3. Remember you will need to secure your camera from the spray of water. You may also need to wear a raincoat and an umbrella will be an added advantage if you do not want the thrill of water drenching you.

This cataract is so called the Devil's cataract due to the dangerous nature of the slope which are undermined with strong currents. Remember not to go beyond the barriers as the ground may not be strong enough to support you. However, if you keep to the trails, you are safe and you may take as many pictures and videos as you can from a safe and secure point.

The vegetation is characterised by long leafy creepers and tall thick trees. This is the ideal temperature creepers and trees need to flourish. The air is cool with a normal humidity in spite of the spray from the falls. Remember to obey the safety warnings. Do not get overwhelmed with the splendour and ignore the safety warnings. Obey the warnings for safety reasons.

Cataract Island view is restricted by a continuous spray of water rising from the falls as white clouds raining down. When the spray is minimal, the view will be clearer. The **Main Falls** can be seen as a large volume of water falling down into the gorge sending up a large cloud of mist. It is a spectacular view not to be missed. Take a video to store for your long lasting memories.

Arm Chair Falls will be seen immediately after the main falls. This may be difficult to appreciate when the water levels are very high. So called Armchair because of the appearance like a the old fashioned armchair. This can be seen east of Livingstone island.

These shapes are made by the force of water cutting through the rocks and the process is actually dynamic. The shapes we are seeing today will not be there tomorrow. Other viewers will identify other shapes and people should feel free to lookout for more shapes and name them accordingly.

Livingstone Island View

This can be seen at position 4 and 5 if the visibility is good. At this position, the island is right in front across the falls. If the spray is too much to make viewing difficult, move to the next point and you will probably see it much clearer. When the water volumes are very high, even this may not be possible. In any case, enjoy the spray.

The island is between the Armchair and Horse shoe falls. It can easily be identified by having no water up-to the edge of the falls. It is the position that is relatively dry. Going to the edge to try and have a clearer view is not recommended for safety reasons.

Likewise it may also be difficult to capture pictures because of the spray. Move between the two positions and take your time to allow the spray to clear and then quickly remove your camera from the plastic bag and take pictures.

This is the island where David Livingstone viewed the Victoria Falls. Access to the island can only be done safely from up stream. Even this is not recommended. During the time of David Livingstone's visit, the Victoria Falls Bridge was not there and access through the trail must have been challenging. The forest had very thick bushes, creepers hanging from trees with wet and slippery rocks, it must have been dangerous and challenging to undertake the trip.

The Danger point

This is the long strip of land coming nearest to the Zambian side. The characteristic feature is that it is slippery and the edges are steep. It rains from the spray of water constantly. Visibility is slightly reduced and signs on the trail are clearly marked.

Keep to the trail and you will have nothing to fear or worry about. Keep your electronic gadgets secured in water proof bags. To the far end of the trail, you can watch the bungee jumpers jumping off the Victoria falls bridge hanging upside down viewing the falls in the "Bat's" position.

End of the Western Cataracts

At this point you have come to the end of the set of the western cataract and viewing points. The return walking trail takes you back to the entrance by passing through the rich foliage of creepers, indigenous trees and grass. This scenery is endowed with its own beauty, unruffled by man or wild game. Protected by the local wildlife regulations and fencing.

Lunar Night View of the Falls

This is viewing of the falls at night specially organized when there is a full moon and subject to good weather; no cloud cover. Extra precaution on safety should be taken as this is night viewing. When you are in Livingstone or Victoria falls town at the gate entrance of the falls, there is a calendar of dates when this is possible.

The Sunset View of the Falls

As the sun sets, you can take this opportunity to look at the falls and setting sun viewing points. These are:

1. The Viewing platform
2. The Viewing Tree
3. The Victoria falls bridge
5. Viewing from the sky

The viewing tree gives the best view at sunset. Extra care should be taken as this involves climbing a set of stair case. If your night sight is not good, this view is not recommended as you may miss a step and injure yourself. Apart from this the viewing should be perfect.

You can also take opportunity to take pictures of the beautiful view of the sun setting from the viewing tree.

The Flora of the Victoria Falls

If your love for flora is anything to talk about, spend the rest of the trail as you walk back to the main entrance watching the trees and vegetation. There is a lot to talk about when looking at trees, grass, shrubs and fungi growing on rocks. These plants should be protected not because they have rights to live but because they remove toxic gases from the atmosphere on our behalf and produce oxygen for our life.

The Falls is fenced to keep elephants from destroying the vegetation but man has been known to be the worst destroyer of the environment by indiscriminate throwing of rubbish, especially plastic. Please avoid throwing rubbish anyhow. Use bins provided.

Animals of the Victoria Falls

Animals of the Victoria falls, though fenced in the Mosi oa Tunya National park which is along the Zambezi river extending to the falls on the Zambian side and the Zambezi national park on the Zimbabwean side, also extending to the Victoria falls, are seen near the falls but can be better watched in the national parks. The visit to the falls is not complete until you pay a visit to the parks to view the animals.

Elephants cross over the borders to graze wherever the grass appears green and in the evening walk down to drink water on the banks of the Zambezi river. They always move in a group. Remember these are not tamed. Do not attack them or try to disturb them. If they are crossing your path, give way. They do not have predators except from poachers.

Buffaloes also move in a group with the young usually in the middle of the pack, although they do not have predators in the park, they still behave like they are deep in the wild. They are also susceptible to poaching.

Impalas will also be seen grazing in a flock usually in grassland. They avoid places where there are tall trees. They have good vision and excellent hearing with speed exceeding 65km/hour. Fortunately for them, they only have man as their predator. They multiply very fast doubling their population in twelve months.

Zebras will be seen walking majestically with white and black stripes across the body. They are pure herbivores and will be seen grazing all the time. They will be seen in a flock and move down to the banks of the Zambezi river in the evenings.

Hippos are numerous, they are nocturnal eaters, grazing at night and swimming in the river during the days, masters of the water. They make a characteristic noise at night.

Warthogs are numerous and can easily be identified by what we call rare 'antenna'. The antenna is actually the tail popping up straight up as the animal flees from danger. They also multiplying fast as predators are few in the park.

Giraffes with their long necks and beautiful brown spots will be seen eating from the top of the acacia trees. They have a characteristic majestic walk. They also do not have predators in the parks and multiply freely.

Birds viewing requires its own book. The great number of species cannot be seen in one hour or one day. Take two or three days to watch and take pictures of birds to appreciate these small but wise creatures. Take time to understand them and you will appreciate life from a different angle. Numerous species of birds will be discussed in detail in separate book.

Other Points of Interest

After all has been viewed and said, you may be interested in going into depth to understand the culture, history of Livingstone and the people around here, take two or three hours to visit the Livngstone Museum. Details of David Livingstone's life and journeys are found in the museum. Political history of Zambia and cultures of the people living in Zambia are all displaced and with a guided tour, your visit will be worthwhile.

Gorge swing for the young at heart is another adventure that you may want to try. The directions are that you turn right just before you reach the **Lookout tree**. The swing is located on one of the gorges of the falls.

A visit to the Crocodile farm will help you understand these reptiles. This is usually a guided tour. The visit can be timed to coincide with the feeding day. Prior enquiry will help you make most of the visit.

The Mukuni village is another place worth spending time. It is the official residence of the Chief of the Toka Leya who are the indigenous people of the Victoria falls area. Proceed straight on by passing the Lookout tree via the paved road you will be at the village and one of the guides will take you in and detail of the culture, life and historical aspects of the people will be explained to you.

Why not conclude your visit with a Sunset cruise on the Zambezi river. Take one of the several cruises on either the Zambian or Zimbabwean side and relax as you watch the sun setting. Prepare your camera for that beautiful picture of the sun setting. You will surely have another opportunity of viewing animals as they come down the Zambezi to take their evening drink before dark sets in.

Finale...

You can visit the falls in any of the many ways. If you are attending a conference or meeting in any place in Zambia or Zimbabwe, take a day or two before or after the conference or meeting to visit. Hire a car and drive yourself or get a driver to Livingstone or Victoria falls town. Get in touch with Zambia Tourism Board or The Zimbabwe Tourism Board to find out about these places and how much they will cost you. Book a room at one of the hotels or lodges. The rest will be history as the saying goes!

GLOSSARY

'Bat's view'	View of the falls while hanging upside down on a bungee rope
Bird's view	View of the Falls from the sky e.g. from a helicopter
'Boiling pot'	The place where water swirls around as it meets rock this is below the Victoria falls bridge.
Chief Mukuni	The traditional leader of the Toka Leya people of Livingstone
Eastern Cataracts	The Cataracts on the Zambian side
Fauna	Animal life
Flora	Plants and vegetation
Head land	The island connected to the main land by the Knife edge bridge. Also called the Knife edge island.
Lunar	Moon
Mukuni Village	The official residence of Chief Mukuni
Mosi –oa-Tunya	The smoke that thunders, local name of the Victoria falls
Northern Rhodesia	Present day Zambia
Palm Groove Trail	Walking trail leading to the Boiling pot
Southern Rhodesia	Present day Zimbabwe
Toka leya	The natives tribe of the Victoria falls
Western Cataracts	The cataract on the Zimbabwean side
Zambezi river	The river that carries the water to the falls

Contact Details

1. Concerning tourism in Zambia and visit to the falls: Zambia National Tourism Board

2. Concerning tourism in Zimbabwe and the visit to the falls: Zimbabwe National Tourism Board

3. Concerning travel to the falls or around Zambia: Tozema Enterprises (www.tozema.com)

4. Game parks in Zambia: Zambia Wild Life Authority (ZAWA)

5. Visa requirements in Zambia: Immigration of Zambia

6. Visa requirements in Zimbabwe: Immigration of Zimbabwe